WILDLIFE WORLDS

NORTH
AMERICA

Tim Harris

D1580687

W
FRANKLIN WATTS
LONDON • SYDNEY

Franklin Watts

First published in Great Britain in 2019 by The Watts Publishing Group

Copyright © The Watts Publishing Group, 2019

HB ISBN: 978 1 4451 6729 9

PB ISBN: 978 1 4451 6730 5

Printed in Dubai

Series Editor: Amy Pimperton

Series Designer: Nic Davies smartdesignstudio.co.uk

Picture researchers: Rachelle Morris (Nature Picture Library),

Laura Sutherland (Nature Picture Library), Diana Morris

Picture credits:

Alamy: David E.Lester 9tl.

Dreamstime: Atomazul 10bl; Anthony Heflin 22c, 31; Irina Kozhemyakina 13bl;
Brian Lasenby 19tr; Michal Pešata 21bl; Andrei Gabriel Stanescu 18.

Nature PL: Ingo Arndt 2b, 10–11c,11bl, 20–21c, 21tr; John Cancalosi 7t, 23tr. Philippe Clement 13tr, 18bl; Claudio Contrera 19tl; Michael Durham 25tr; David Fleetham 15tl; Dr Axel Gebauer back cover tr,7bl; Danny Green front cover t; Gavin Hellier 26–27c; Daniel Heuclin 17c; Ole Jorgen Liodden 29c; Barry Mansell 19bl; Larry Michael 23c; Flip Nicklin 28bl; Todd Pusser 27tl; Jouan Rius 6b, 12, 17tl; Charlie Summers 27br; Tom Vezo back cover tl, 9cl, 13tl; Gerrit Vyn 8–9p; Doc White 28c.

Shutterstock: Ad-hominem 5c; James Anderson 27bl, 32b; Bildagenteur Zoonar GmbH 5b; Bill45 6t, 16; Bobs Creek Photography 25t, 32t; miroslav chytil back cover tcr, 4b; Dydo Diem 10t; Rudi Ernst 3b, 13br; FotoRequest 11br, 29tl; C_Gara 29bl; Karin de Jonge-Fotografie 29tr; Chris Kolaczan 26bl; Alex Krassel 15tr; Brian Lasenby 21br; Viktor Loki 7br; magnusdeepbelow 15br; Maria Martyshova front cover c, 1c; Joe McDonald 9cr; MNStudio 3t, 14–15c; Steve Oehlenschlager 21cr; David Osborn 1t, 25br; Bill Perry 3bg, 4–5c, 6t, 32c; PhotoXite 2t, 24–25c; Tom Reichner 3c, 17br, 20l; Nancy S 19br, 30t; Sezai Sahmay back cover tcl, 14bl; Steven Russell Smit front cover b; Jenn Strong 5t; Paul Tessier 23tl; Vara I 24bl; Sista Vongjuntanaruk 8bl; Joe West 15bl, 30b.

With thanks to the Nature Picture Library

Franklin Watts

An imprint of

Hachette Children's Group

Part of The Watts Publishing Group

Carmelite House

50 Victoria Embankment

London EC4Y 0DZ

An Hachette UK Company

www.hachette.co.uk

www.franklinwatts.co.uk

Contents

North American Continent

North America is Earth's third largest continent, after Asia and Africa. In the far south-east, a narrow strip of land called the Isthmus of Panama connects it to South America, but otherwise it is surrounded by ocean.

In the far north, Greenland is permanently covered by a thick ice sheet, and there are many glaciers in the Rocky Mountains. In contrast, Costa Rica, Honduras and Panama have tropical rainforests, and major deserts stretch across northern Mexico and the south-western US. Coniferous forest covers much of Canada, while the gentle Appalachian Mountains are cloaked with broadleaved woodland.

In such a continent of contrasts, it is not surprising that North America is renowned for amazing wildlife spectacles. These include grizzly bears hunting salmon as they swim up rivers in Alaska, millions of bats emerging at dusk from caves in Texas, and thousands of herons feeding with basking alligators in the Florida Everglades.

GREY WOLF

Snow-covered Denali, in Alaska, is the highest mountain in North America at 6,190 metres.

GRIZZLY BEAR

ARCTIC OCEAN

GREENLAND

Baffin Island

Alaska

ARCTIC CIRCLE

GULF OF ALASKA

LABRADOR SEA

NORTH PACIFIC OCEAN

CANADA

HUDSON BAY

Rocky Mountains

Banff National Park

NORTH ATLANTIC OCEAN

Yellowstone National Park

Great Lakes

5

Prairies

2

4

Great Lakes: 1. Erie;
2. Huron; 3. Michigan;
4. Ontario; 5. Superior

Redwood Forests

MISSISSIPPI RIVER

3

1

Monument Valley

COLORADO RIVER

Badlands National Park

Appalachians

Shenandoah National Park

Mojave Desert

Grand Canyon

Mount Elbert

USA

Blue Ridge Mountains

HAWAII

Mauna Loa

Mississippi River Delta

Everglades

MEXICO

GULF OF MEXICO

BELIZE

HONDURAS

In the Midwest, where once millions of bison roamed over natural prairie grassland, arable farmland now stretches to the horizon in every direction.

GUATEMALA

EL SALVADOR

NICARAGUA

COSTA RICA

PANAMA

SOUTH PACIFIC OCEAN

AMERICAN ALLIGATOR

Mojave Desert

The Mojave Desert is a land of rolling sand dunes, rugged mountains and rocky country covered with creosote bushes and Joshua trees. One area, Death Valley, is the lowest, hottest and driest place in North America.

Coyotes are nocturnal, emerging each evening to hunt. Then, their howling calls are heard. Jackrabbits and other small animals shelter under bushes or hide in burrows to avoid the Sun's heat. Desert tortoises sleep through the whole of the summer heat, waking only when the weather gets cooler in autumn.

DEATH VALLEY

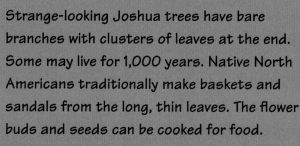

Strange-looking Joshua trees have bare branches with clusters of leaves at the end. Some may live for 1,000 years. Native North Americans traditionally make baskets and sandals from the long, thin leaves. The flower buds and seeds can be cooked for food.

Roadrunners rarely fly, but they can run quicker than the fastest human sprinter. Their favourite meals include spiders, scorpions and lizards.

Hungry sand scorpions leave their holes at night in search of food. They are the largest scorpion species in North America.

The throat of a Costa's hummingbird shines brilliant purple in sunlight. This little bird feeds on the nectar of desert flowers.

Mississippi River

The third longest river in the world is the mighty Mississippi. It flows 3,730 kilometres from Lake Itasca in Minnesota, south to the Gulf of Mexico. Just before it reaches the sea, it splits into many different channels.

Other large rivers, such as the Missouri, Ohio and Arkansas, join forces with the Mississippi before it reaches the sea. People have used it as a transportation route for thousands of years. Almost 400 kinds of fish live in its waters, along with freshwater turtles, alligators and waterbirds.

Snapping turtles lie in wait for their prey in shallow, muddy water.

Water from 31 states drains into the Mississippi as it meanders through forests, farmland and big cities such as Memphis and New Orleans. Close to the sea, the Mississippi River Delta contains salt flats, such as those found in Barataria Bay (above).

Green darner dragonflies fly over the river, chasing and eating smaller insects.

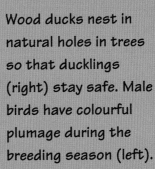

Wood ducks nest in natural holes in trees so that ducklings (right) stay safe. Male birds have colourful plumage during the breeding season (left).

Everglades

In southern Florida, the Everglades is a wetland so large that it is impossible to see from one side to the other. Despite its size, its water is so shallow that it would only come up to an average adult's knees.

Millions of fish and other small creatures live in its waters. They attract predators. Thousands of herons wade through the water, snatching fish with their beaks. Menacing alligators patrol, in search of larger prey. Mangrove forests grow where the fresh water of the Everglades meets the ocean. Offshore, manatees swim in the shallows, grazing on underwater plants.

River otters are playful animals covered in thick, velvety fur. They swim superbly when chasing fish.

The Everglades attract thousands of herons, including green herons, (right), egrets and ibis, which feed in the shallows.

The vast sawgrass marshes of the Everglades are sometimes called the 'River of Grass'.

An American alligator slowly drifts through the shallows, with only its head showing above water as it looks for a meal.

Grand Canyon

The most massive canyon in North America cuts through northern Arizona as if a giant knife had sliced through Earth's surface. It is more than 400 kilometres long and in some places it is 25 kilometres wide.

For more than 6 million years, the Colorado River has been cutting down through the rocks of the Colorado Plateau, exposing layers of older and older rock as it has eroded the canyon. Rocks in the bottom of the gorge are nearly 2 billion years old.

The Grand Canyon is so deep that it would take six Eiffel Towers stacked one on top of the other to reach from bottom to top. In many places, the canyon walls are vertical. This is where the hardest rocks are. Gentler slopes have formed where there are softer rocks.

The venom of a black widow spider is powerful enough to kill many small animals.

Mountain lions, or cougars, are active mostly at night.

The bald eagle is the national bird of the USA. These magnificent birds of prey hunt trout in the Colorado River.

Clever camouflage makes horned lizards difficult to see against rocks.

Hawaii

Hawaii is one of a group of islands in the middle of the Pacific Ocean. It is built on five volcanoes. Between October and April, very heavy rain falls on the islands. Hawaii is one of the wettest places on Earth.

Rainforest grows on the lower slopes of the volcanoes. Some of the forest birds live nowhere else in the world. The ocean water around Hawaii is very rich in marine life, including sea turtles, monk seals, dolphins, humpback whales and many different kinds of fish.

One of Hawaii's volcanoes – Mauna Loa – is the largest volcano on Earth. Another, Kilauea, has erupted almost continuously since 1983, sending molten lava streaming down its slopes. The lava cools and becomes hard. After a few years, plants begin to grow on it.

Pom-pom crabs hold sea anemones in their claws. The anemones gather tiny particles of food, which the crab scrapes off and then eats.

The nene is the world's rarest goose. In the wild, it lives only on Hawaii and its neighbouring islands.

Although it looks scary, the giant oceanic manta ray is a harmless fish.

Hawaiian hibiscus, or *ma'o-hau-hele*, grows up to 10 metres tall and has bright yellow flowers.

Monument Valley

On the border of Arizona and Utah huge stacks of sandstone rock, called buttes, rise high above the red desert of Monument Valley. The red colouration comes from chemicals in the rocks.

In summer, the valley is very hot, but it can be cold enough for snow to settle in winter. At first sight it may look lifeless, but many lizards, jackrabbits and other creatures live there. They are hunted by predators, such as red-tailed hawks, mountain lions and rattlesnakes.

West Mitten Butte (left) and East Mitten Butte (right) tower about 300 metres above the valley floor. These huge chunks of rock are so named because they look like gigantic mittens.

Leopard lizards have spots like leopards. These small desert reptiles warm themselves by sunbathing on rocks. Juveniles like this one have brightly coloured spots.

Venomous rattlesnakes scare away their enemies by shaking the hollow scales at the end of their tail. When shaken, these make a rattling noise.

Soapweed yuccas can survive the very dry conditions in Monument Valley. Native North Americans boil the plant's seeds for food.

Redwood Forest

The lush forests that grow near the coast of the Pacific Ocean in northern California have the world's tallest trees. They are called coastal redwoods.

The tallest of all these trees, named Hyperion, was discovered in 2006. At 115 metres, it is taller than the dome of St Paul's Cathedral. The redwood forest and the rivers that run through it are home to many animals, some of which are rare. They include the northern spotted owl and the Chinook salmon.

The redwoods thrive in the very wet forest. Heavy rains fall during the winter and fog rolls in from the ocean in summer. Unlike tropical rainforest, it is cool for much of the year – but it is just as wet!

During the day, Townsend's big-eared bats sleep in caves and old buildings. They wake up at dusk to hunt for flying insects.

Nocturnal flying squirrels can glide from tree to tree when they need to. They are equally adapted for climbing tree trunks and leaping among the branches.

Ring-necked snakes live on the forest floor. They show their bright underbelly to warn off predators.

In the breeding season, male Sierran treefrogs gather by water and call to attract females.

Prairies

Once, an immense 'sea' of grass stretched across most of the American Midwest. Only a fraction of that natural grassland – called prairies – now remains.

Most of the prairies have been converted to fields of wheat or maize (corn), or for cattle ranching. What remains is short-grass prairie in the west. In the wetter east, long-grass prairie grows taller than a person, with a 'carpet' of wildflowers beneath. The prairies were once the home of millions of bison, but only a few thousand of these huge grazing animals remain.

American bison (buffalo) graze on prairie grasses. They spend their days grazing, resting, chewing the cud, then looking for new places to munch grass.

Small purple and yellow pasque flowers are the first sign of spring on the prairies, sometimes poking up through snow.

Over thousands of years, the soft rocks beneath the prairie of Badlands National Park have been worn away by the action of rivers and streams. This erosion has created a dramatic landscape of pinnacles and gullies. There are millions of fossils in these rocks, including ancient horses and alligators.

Mixed-grass prairie grows at Badlands. These places in the central portion of the prairie are where short grass and long grass meet.

In April, male prairie chickens inflate yellow air sacs on their necks to attract females.

When wildflowers bloom on the South Dakota prairie, orange-and-black monarch butterflies come to feed on milkweed.

Blue Ridge Mountains

The Blue Ridge Mountains form part of the Appalachian range. There are 125 peaks more than 1,500 metres high and the mountains stretch from Alabama in the south to Pennsylvania in the north. Broadleaf and conifer forest covers the summits.

Bears, foxes, coyotes, bobcats, deer and snakes live beneath the trees. In spring, the songs of thousands of birds echo through the forest. Salamanders and frogs swim in the many streams that flow towards the Great Appalachian Valley on one side and the Atlantic Ocean on the other.

The blue haze that gives the mountains their name sits over the forested ridges of Shenandoah National Park. A chemical given off by the trees produces the colour.

Only male wild turkeys have the magnificent, fan-shaped tail. They are heavy birds, but fly well through the forest and often perch high in trees.

Since the tiny Shenandoah salamander needs damp conditions to thrive, it lives only in the higher, wetter parts of the mountains.

Bobcats have tufted ears and a stubby tail. They go hunting for small animals at twilight in the morning and evening.

Yellowstone National Park

Towering fountains of boiling water, mud pools, colourful hot springs, spectacular waterfalls and steep-sided canyons can all be seen in Yellowstone. This national park in Wyoming is a vast area of natural wilderness.

Fascinating animals live in the dark pine forests, grasslands and lakes of Yellowstone. There are lumbering bison, bears and elk (moose), herds of wild horses and hunting wolves, mountain lions and wolverines. Eagles, hawks and many other birds make their homes in this, the oldest national park in North America.

Every hour or so, and with a loud whooshing sound, the Old Faithful Geyser shoots boiling water 40 metres into the air. Since it was first discovered in 1870 it has erupted more than one million times.

Herds of wild mustang horses roam across the park's grasslands.

The vivid colours of Grand Prismatic Spring are created by millions of bacteria.

Wolves were reintroduced to Yellowstone in the 1990s and are now thriving, with about a dozen packs ranging through its forests.

Elk are the world's largest deer. The males use their gigantic antlers to fight each other.

Rocky Mountains

Hundreds of peaks make up North America's greatest mountain range, which stretches 4,800 kilometres from New Mexico to British Columbia. The tallest of them is Mount Elbert, in Colorado, which rises 4,400 metres above sea level.

The lower slopes are cloaked in forest. Higher, there are meadows, which in spring are alive with wildflowers and butterflies. Bighorn sheep, deer and marmots also live there. The highest summits are bare rock and support little life. Rivers tumble down the steep slopes and crash over waterfalls. Lakes lie in the bottom of deep valleys that were carved by glaciers.

Few animals live on the highest mountains, but sure-footed bighorn sheep can clamber up the steep, rocky slopes.

Grizzly bears have a fearsome reputation but are happy to eat nuts, grass and flowers, as well as hunt animals.

Beautifully patterned tiger salamanders live in water when they are young, then leave to live among fallen leaves and soil.

Snow-dusted mountains tower over the still waters of Peyto Lake, in Banff National Park. Sediment in the water gives the lake its bright turquoise hue. The first national park established in Canada, Banff has glaciers, hot springs, deep caves and coniferous forests.

Greenback cut-throat trout thrive only in clean streams with calm pools.

Baffin Island

Baffin Island in north-east Canada is the world's fifth-largest island. There is permanent daylight in midsummer, but the Sun does not rise at all from November to the end of January.

The island is bitterly cold and the temperature stays mostly below freezing. Inland, the treeless tundra landscape is too harsh for people to live, but there are herds of reindeer and many lemmings, Arctic hares and Arctic foxes. Seabirds nest on coastal cliffs. Below, polar bears and walruses hunt and rest on the frozen ocean.

Beluga, or white, whales are very sociable animals. Dozens or even hundreds swim around together as they search for crustaceans or shoals of fish to eat.

A snowy owl's black and white feathers blend in with the snow-covered ground.

'Seas' of cottongrass flower on the tundra each spring.

Polar bears are huge carnivores whose favourite food is seals. The bears are excellent swimmers.

Their white winter fur makes Arctic hares difficult for predators to see. In summer, they have brown fur.

Glossary

antlers branched horns on a deer's head

arable land used for crops

bacteria single-celled micro-organisms that often cause diseases

camouflage colouration that makes an animal hard to see in its natural surroundings

carnivores animals that kill and eat other animals

coyote a wolf-like wild dog

crustaceans animals with an external skeleton but no backbone, such as a lobster or crab

delta the area where a river drops its sediment as it enters a lake or the ocean

desert a place that receives little or no rainfall and has few plants or none at all

eroded worn away by the action of rain, waves and wind

geyser a hot spring where boiling water causes jets of water and steam to erupt

glaciers a large body of ice moving slowly down a valley

hibernate to spend the winter in a deep sleep

iceberg a large mass of floating ice that has broken away from a glacier

juvenile a young animal

lava hot, molten rock that erupts from a volcano

manatee an aquatic plant-eating mammal; sea cow

mangrove trees and shrubs that grow in coastal swamps

nectar sugary liquid found in flowers

nocturnal active at night

permanent something that is present all the time

plateau high, level ground

plumage a bird's feathers

predators animals that hunt and kill other animals

prey animals that are eaten by other animals

rainforest dense forests with high amounts of rainfall

sandstone sedimentary rock made of sand or quartz grains that have been compressed together

sea anemone a sea animal that has a ring of stinging tentacles around its mouth

sediment tiny grains of rock in water

shoals big groups of fish

sociable liking the company of others

summit the very top

tundra a flat, treeless region of the Arctic

venom a chemical some animals use to poison prey

venomous producing chemicals that can injure or kill prey

vertical straight up

Books

Animal Families (series) by Tim Harris (Wayland, 2014)
Close-up Continents: Mapping North America by Paul Rockett (Franklin Watts, 2016)
If Polar Bears Disappeared by Lily Williams (Wayland, 2019)
Natural Wonders of the World by Molly Oldfield (Wren & Rook, 2019)

Websites

Kidzone Geography: Rocky Mountains
Lots of information about the geography, plants, and animals of North America's greatest mountain range.
www.kidzone.ws/habitats/rocky-mountains.htm

Mississippi River
The history and geography of the great river.
www.coolkidfacts.com/mississippi-river/

National Geographic Animal Pictures and Facts
Simply type in the animals you're interested in, and get lots of fascinating facts. Covers mammals, reptiles, amphibians, fish and birds.
www.nationalgeographic.com/animals/index/

National Park Service: Everglades
Information about the history, people, nature, and geography of Florida's Everglades.
www.nps.gov/ever/learn/kidsyouth/learning-about-the-everglades.htm

North America Facts for Kids
Fun facts about the continent of North America.
www.kids-world-travel-guide.com/north-america-facts.html

Note to parents and teachers: Every effort has been made by the Publishers to ensure that the websites in this book are of the highest educational value, and that they contain no inappropriate or offensive material. However, because of the nature of the Internet, it is impossible to guarantee that the contents of these sites will not be altered. We strongly advise that Internet access is supervised by a responsible adult.

Further information

Index